The Testament of Moses

By Moses

Copyright © 2020 Lamp of Trismegistus. All rights reserved. No part of this publication may be reproduced or transmitted in any form or by any means, electronic or mechanical, including photocopying, recording, or by any information storage and retrieval system, without permission in writing from Lamp of Trismegistus. Reviewers may quote brief passages.

ISBN: 978-1-63118-440-6

Christian Apocrypha Series

Other Books in this Series and Related Titles

The Testament of Abraham by Abraham (978-1-63118-441-3)

Book of Dreams by Enoch (978-1-63118-437-6)

Psalms of Solomon by King Solomon (978-1-63118-439-0)

The Lives of Adam and Eve by Moses (978-1-63118-414-7)

The First and Second Gospels of the Infancy of Jesus Christ by Thomas and James (978-1-63118-415-4)

Lost Chapters of the Book of Daniel and Related Writings by Daniel (978-1-63118-417-8)

The Book of Astronomical Secrets by Enoch (978-1-63118-443-7)

The Book of the Watchers by Enoch (978-1-63118-416-1)

The Book of Parables by Enoch (978-1-63118-429-1)

Masonic Symbolism of Easter and the Christ in Masonry by various authors (978-1-63118-434-5)

A Few Masonic Sermons by A. C. Ward & Bascom B. Clarke (978-1-63118-435-2)

Masonic Symbolism of King Solomon's Temple by Albert G. Mackey & others (978-1-63118-442-0)

Cloud Upon the Sanctuary by A. E. Waite & K. Eckartshausen (978-1-63118-438-3)

The Two Great Pillars of Boaz and Jachin by Albert G. Mackey & others (978-1-63118-433-8)

Audio Versions are also Available on Audible and iTunes

Table of Contents

Introduction...7

Prologue...11

Chapter I...15

Chapter II...17

Chapter III...19

Chapter IV...21

Chapter V...23

Chapter VI...25

Chapter VII...27

Chapter VIII...29

Chapter XIX...31

Chapter X...33

Chapter XI...35

Chapter XII...39

Introduction

The Apocrypha are a loosely knit series of books, written by early vanguards of Christianity (covering the eras of both the old and new testaments), and which comprise somewhere between about a dozen to several hundred titles, depending on whom you ask and how that person defines "Apocrypha." A small selection of these can still be found included in the Catholic bible, while a majority of the books in question, were abandoned by church officials in the early centuries of Christianity. Many of these apocryphal books were originally considered canon by early followers of Christ, in the first four centuries following his birth. It wasn't until the meeting of the Council of Nicaea in 325, that Emperor Constantine and a group of roughly 300 church bishops, gathered together with the goal of defining, standardizing and unifying an otherwise splintering Christianity, that many of these writings ceased to be included in the newly established canon. Enjoy then, this book as an example, of just one of the many books of the Christian Apocrypha, and be sure to check out other titles in this series.

PROLOGUE

The Testament of Moses, sometimes called by the title The Assumption of Moses, is one of the flagship pieces of apocalyptic biblical literature.

The original text of this piece is considered to date to the very early first century, with some scholars dating it even earlier; however, the more common and more complete Latin version, on which this translation was based, is known to be a sixth century document.

Here is what translator R. H. Charles has to say about the date, in his original translation, as well as some commonalties between this text and the canonical bible:

> *The Assumption of Moses was, in all probability, a composite work, and consisted of two originally distinct books, of which the first was really the Testament of Moses, and the second the Assumption. The former was written in Hebrew, between 7 and 29 A.D., and possibly also the latter. A Greek version of the entire work appeared in the first century A.D. Of this a few phrases and sentences have been preserved in St. Matt. xxiv. 29; Acts vii. 35 and St. Jude 9, 16 and 18.*

As for the content, the text is a series of secret messages and instructions, which Moses reveals to Joshua, prior to the act of passing leadership of the Israelites on to him, and it includes apocalyptic descriptions in addition to other prophecies. Some parts, such as chapter 7, are fragmented, making it difficult to understand what is happening, and the manuscript itself ends abruptly, indicating there was originally more there. Still, however, this is a fascinating look at one small piece of a larger, rich history of the myths surrounding Moses.

The book comes to us is in the form of an address, specifically one that was delivered by Moses to Joshua. In this address, there is a description of how Moses, just at the moment when he is about to die, delivers to Joshua a collection of the sacred writings, which he had been given. Moses then reveals, to his successor, the prophecies which he had been instructed to keep a record of, but which, at the same time, he had been instructed to hide away, until a predetermined point in time which specifically concerned the Hebrew nation as a whole. An overview of the history of the Jewish people, up to the author's time is described. He tells of how one tribe shall say to another:

> "Lo, is not this that which Moses did once declare unto us in prophecies? Yea, he declared and called heaven and earth to witness against us that we should not transgress the commandments of the Lord, of which he was the mediator to us."

There are also some references to the destruction of Jerusalem in the year 587 B.C., the persecution of Antiochus, the rule of the Hasmoneans, the divisions between Pharisees and Sadducees, as well as the reign of Herod. Finally, however, the book eventually ends on an optimistic note, for the promise of a happy future is given; this is a fairly common manner in which these types of apocalyptic books of this era come to an end.

Like nearly all texts of the biblical Apocrypha, the original author of this text has been lost to time; however, R. H. Charles prepared this particular translation, in 1897.

Chapter I

And it came to pass in the one hundred and twentieth year of the life of Moses,

That is, the two thousand five hundredth year from the creation of the world,

That he called to him Joshua the son of Nun, a man approved of the Lord,

That he might be the minister of the people and of the tabernacle of the testimony with all its holy things,

And that he might bring the people into the land given to their fathers,

That it should be given to them according to the covenant and the oath, which he spake in the tabernacle to give it by Joshua: saying to Joshua these words:

"Be strong and of a good courage according to thy might so as to do what has been commanded that thou mayest be blameless unto God."

So saith the Lord of the world.

For He hath created the world on behalf of His people.

But He was not pleased to manifest this purpose of creation from the foundation of the world, in order that the Gentiles might thereby be convicted, yea to their own humiliation might by their arguments convict one another.

Accordingly He designed and devised me, and He prepared me before the foundation of the world, that I should be the mediator of His covenant.

And now I declare unto thee that the time of the years of my life is fulfilled and I am passing away to sleep with my fathers even in the presence of all the people.

And receive thou this writing that thou mayest know how to preserve the books which I shall deliver unto thee:

And thou shalt set these in order and anoint them with oil of cedar and put them away in earthen vessels in the place which He made from the beginning of the creation of the world,

That His name should be called upon until the day of repentance in the visitation where with the Lord shall visit them in the consummation of the end of the days.

Chapter II

And now they shall go by means of thee into the land which He determined and promised to give to their fathers,

In the which thou shalt bless and give to them individually and confirm unto them their inheritance in me and establish for them the kingdom, and thou shalt appoint them prefectures according to the good pleasure of their Lord in judgment and righteousness.

And it shall come to pass in the sixth year after they enter into the land, that thereafter they shall be ruled by chiefs and kings for eighteen years, and during nineteen years the ten tribes shall break away.

And the twelve tribes shall go down and transfer the tabernacle of the testimony. Then the God of heaven will make the court of His tabernacle and the tower of His sanctuary, and the two holy tribes shall be there established:

but the ten tribes shall establish kingdoms for themselves according to their own ordinances.

And they shall offer sacrifices throughout twenty years:

and seven shall entrench the walls, and I will protect nine, but four shall transgress the covenant of the Lord, and profane the oath which the Lord made with them.

And they shall sacrifice their sons to strange gods, and they shall set up idols in the sanctuary, to worship them.

And in the house of the Lord they shall work impiety and engrave every form of beast, even many abominations.

Chapter III

And in those days a king from the east shall come against them and his cavalry shall cover their land.

And he shall burn their colony with fire together with the holy temple of the Lord, and he shall carry away all the holy vessels.

And he shall cast forth all the people, and he shall take them to the land of his nativity, yea he shall take the two tribes with him.

Then the two tribes shall call upon the ten tribes, and shall march as a lioness on the dusty plains, being hungry and thirsty.

And they shall cry aloud: 'Righteous and holy is the Lord, for, inasmuch as ye have sinned, we too, in like manner, have been carried away with you, together with our children."

Then the ten tribes shall mourn on hearing the reproaches of the two tribes.

And they shall say: 'What have we done unto you, brethren? Has not this tribulation come on all the house of Israel?'

And all the tribes shall mourn, crying unto heaven and saying:

'God of Abraham God of Isaac and God of Jacob, remember Thy covenant which Thou didst make with them, and the oath which Thou didst swear unto them by Thyself, that their seed should never fail from the land which Thou hast given them.'

Then they shall remember me, saying, in that day, tribe unto tribe and each man unto his neighbor:

'Is not this that which Moses did then declare unto us in prophecies, who suffered many things in Egypt and in the Red Sea and in the wilderness during forty years,

And assuredly called heaven and earth to witness against us, that we should not transgress His commandments, in the which he was a mediator unto us?

Behold these things have befallen us after his death according to his declaration, as he declared to us at that time, yea behold these have taken place even to our being carried away captive into the country of the east.'

Who shall be also in bondage for about seventy and seven years.

Chapter IV

Then there shall enter one who is over them, and he shall spread forth his hands, and kneel upon his knees and pray on their behalf saying:

'Lord of all, King on the lofty throne, who rulest the world, and didst will that this people should be Thine elect people, then indeed Thou didst will that Thou shouldst be called their God, according to the covenant which Thou didst make with their fathers.

And yet they have gone in captivity in another land with their wives and their children, and around the gates of strange peoples and where there is great vanity.

Regard and have compassion on them, O Lord of heaven.'

Then God will remember them on account of the covenant which He made with their fathers, and He will manifest His compassion in those times also.

And He will put it into the mind of a king to have compassion on them, and he shall send them off to their land and country.

Then some portions of the tribes shall go up and they shall come to their appointed place, and they shall anew surround the place with walls.

And the two tribes shall continue in their prescribed faith, sad and lamenting because they will not be able to offer sacrifices to the Lord of their fathers.

And the ten tribes shall increase and multiply among the Gentiles during the time of their captivity.

Chapter V

And when the times of chastisement draw nigh and vengeance arises through the kings who share in their guilt and punish them,

They themselves also shall be divided as to the truth.

Wherefore it hath come to pass: 'They shall turn aside from righteousness and approach iniquity, and they shall defile with pollutions the house of their worship,' and because 'they shall go a-whoring after strange gods.'

For they shall not follow the truth of God, but some shall pollute the altar with the very gifts which they offer to the Lord, who are not priests but slaves, sons of slaves.

And many in those times shall have respect unto desirable persons and receive gifts, and pervert judgment on receiving presents.

And on this account the colony and the borders of their habitation shall be filled with lawless deeds and iniquities: those who wickedly depart from the Lord shall be judges: they shall be ready to judge for money as each may wish.

Chapter VI

Then there shall be raised up unto them kings bearing rule, and they shall call themselves priests of the Most High God: they shall assuredly work iniquity in the holy of holies.

And an insolent king shall succeed them, who will not be of the race of the priests, a man bold and shameless, and he shall judge them as they shall deserve.

And he shall cut off their chief men with the sword, and shall destroy them in secret places, so that no one may know where their bodies are.

He shall slay the old and the young, and he shall not spare.

Then the fear of him shall be bitter unto them in their land.

And he shall execute judgments on them as the Egyptians executed upon them, during thirty and four years, and he shall punish them.

And he shall beget children, who succeeding him shall rule for shorter periods.

Into their parts cohorts and a powerful king of the west shall come, who shall conquer them:.

And he shall take them captive, and burn a part of their temple with fire, and shall crucify some around their colony.

Chapter VII

And when this is done the times shall be ended, in a moment the second course shall be ended, the four hours shall come.

They shall be forced. ...

And, in the time of these, destructive and impious men shall rule, saying that they are just.

And these shall stir up the poison of their minds, being treacherous men, self-pleasers, dissemblers in all their own affairs and lovers of banquets at every hour of the day, gluttons, gourmands.

Devourers of the goods of the poor saying that they do so on the ground of their justice, but in reality to destroy them, complainers, deceitful, concealing themselves lest they should be recognized, impious, filled with lawlessness and iniquity from sunrise to sunset.

Saying: 'We shall have feastings and luxury, eating and drinking, and we shall esteem ourselves as princes.'

And though their hands and their minds touch unclean things, yet their mouth shall speak great things, and they shall say furthermore:

'Do not touch me lest thou shouldst pollute me in the place where I stand.'

Chapter VIII

And there shall come upon them a second visitation and wrath, such as has not befallen them from the beginning until that time, in which He will stir up against them the king of the kings of the earth and one that ruleth with great power, who shall crucify those who confess to their circumcision:

And those who conceal it he shall torture and deliver them up to be bound and led into prison.

And their wives shall be given to the gods among the Gentiles, and their young sons shall be operated on by the physicians in order to bring forward their foreskin.

And others amongst them shall be punished by tortures and fire and sword, and they shall be forced to bear in public their idols, polluted as they are like those who keep them.

And they shall likewise be forced by those who torture them to enter their inmost sanctuary, and they shall be forced by goads to blaspheme with insolence the word, finally after these things the laws and what they had above their altar.

Chapter IX

Then in that day there shall be a man of the tribe of Levi, whose name shall be Taxo, who having seven sons shall speak to them exhorting them:

Observe, my sons, behold a second ruthless and unclean visitation has come upon the people, and a punishment merciless and far exceeding the first.

For what nation or what region or what people of those who are impious towards the Lord, who have done many abominations, have suffered as great calamities as have befallen us?

Now, therefore, my sons, hear me: for observe and know that neither did the fathers nor their forefathers tempt God, so as to transgress His commands.

And ye know that this is our strength, and thus we will do.

Let us fast for the space of three days and on the fourth let us go into a cave which is in the field, and let us die rather than transgress the commands of the Lord of Lords, the God of our fathers.

For if we do this and die, our blood shall be avenged before the Lord.

Chapter X

And then His kingdom shall appear throughout all His creation,
And then Satan shall be no more,

And sorrow shall depart with him.

Then the hands of the angel shall be filled
Who has been appointed chief,
And he shall forthwith avenge them of their enemies.

For the Heavenly One will arise from His royal throne,
And He will go forth from His holy habitation:
And His wrath will burn on account of His sons.

And the earth shall tremble: to its confines shall it be shaken:
And the high mountains shall be made low
And the hills shall be shaken and fall.

And the horns of the sun shall be broken and he shall be turned into darkness;

And the moon shall not give her light, and be turned wholly into blood.

And the circle of the stars shall be disturbed.

And the sea shall retire into the abyss. And the fountains of waters shall fail, And the rivers shall dry up.

For the Most High will arise, the Eternal God alone,
And He will appear to punish the Gentiles,

And He will destroy all their idols.

Then thou, O Israel, shalt be happy,
And thou shalt mount upon the necks and wings of the eagle,
And they shall be ended.

And God will exalt thee,
And He will cause thee to approach to the heaven of the stars,
And He will establish thy habitation among them.

And thou shalt look from on high and shalt see thy enemies in Gehenna,
And thou wilt recognize them and rejoice,
And thou wilt give thanks and confess thy Creator.

And do thou, Joshua the son of Nun, keep these words and this book;

For from my death—my assumption—until His advent there will be CCL times.

And this is the course of the times which they shall pursue till they are consummated.

And I shall go to sleep with my fathers.

Wherefore, Joshua thou son of Nun, be strong and be of good courage; for God hath chosen thee to be my successor in the same covenant.

Chapter XI

And when Joshua had heard the words of Moses that were so written in his writing all that he had before said, he rent his clothes and cast himself at Moses' feet.

And Moses comforted him and wept with him.

And Joshua answered him and said:

'Why dost thou comfort me, my lord Moses? And how shall I be comforted in regard to the bitter word which thou hast spoken which has gone forth from thy mouth, which is full of tears and lamentation, in that thou departest from this people?

But now what place shall receive thee?

Or what shall be the sign that marks thy sepulcher?

Or who shall dare to move thy body from thence as that of a mere man from place to place?

For all men when they die have according to their age their sepulchers on earth; but thy sepulcher is from the rising to the setting sun, and from the south to the confines of the north: all the world is thy sepulcher.

My lord, thou art departing, and who shall feed this people?

Or who is there that shall have compassion on them and who shall be their guide by the way?

Or who shall pray for them, not omitting a single day, in order that I may lead them into the land of their forefathers?

How therefore am I to foster this people as a father his only son, or as a mistress her daughter, a virgin who is being prepared to be given to the husband whom she will revere, while she guards her person from the sun and takes care that her feet are not unshod for running upon the ground.

And how shall I supply them with food and drink according to the pleasure of their will?

For of them there shall be 600,000 men, for these have multiplied to this degree through thy prayers, my lord Moses.

And what wisdom or understanding have I that I should judge or answer by word in the house of the Lord?

And the kings of the Amorites also when they hear that we are attacking them, believing that there is no longer among them the sacred spirit who was worthy of the Lord,

Manifold and incomprehensible, the lord of the word, who was faithful in all things, God's chief prophet throughout the earth, the most perfect teacher in the world, that he is no longer among them, shall say "Let us go against them.

If the enemy have but once wrought impiously against their Lord, they have no advocate to offer prayers on their behalf to the Lord, like Moses the great messenger,

Who every hour day and night had his knees fixed to the earth, praying and looking for help to Him that ruleth all the world with compassion and righteousness, reminding Him of the covenant of the fathers and propitiating the Lord with the oath."

For they shall say: "He is not with them: let us go therefore and destroy them from off the face of the earth."

What shall then become of this people, my lord Moses?'

Chapter XII

And when Joshua had finished these words, he cast himself again at the feet of Moses.

And Moses took his hand and raised him into the seat before him, and answered and said unto him:

"Joshua, do not despise thyself, but set thy mind at ease, and hearken to my words.

All the nations which are in the earth God hath created and us, He hath foreseen them and us from the beginning of the creation of the earth unto the end of the age, and nothing has been neglected by Him even to the least thing, but all things He hath foreseen and caused all to come forth.

Yea all things which are to be in this earth the Lord hath foreseen and lo! they are brought forward into the light ....

The Lord hath on their behalf appointed me to pray for their sins and make intercession for them.

For not for any virtue or strength of mine, but of His good pleasure have His compassion and longsuffering fallen to my lot.

For I say unto you, Joshua: it is not on account of the godliness of this people that thou shalt root out the nations.

The lights of the heaven, the foundations of the earth have been made and approved by God and are under the signet ring of His right hand.

Those, therefore, who do and fulfill the commandments of God shall increase and be prospered:

But those who sin and set at naught the commandments shall be without the blessings before mentioned, and they shall be punished with many torments by the nations.

But wholly to root out and destroy them is not permitted.

For God will go forth who has foreseen all things forever, and His covenant has been established and has His oath.

www.ingramcontent.com/pod-product-compliance
Lightning Source LLC
LaVergne TN
LVHW041502070426
835507LV00009B/774